W9-BXV-716

Capstone

DR 18.49

5/13

I Want a Pet

I Want a Hamster

by Kimberly M. Hutmacher

Consulting Editor: Gail Saunders-Smith, PhD

Consultant: Jennifer Zablotny, DVM
Member, American Veterinary Medical Association

CAPSTONE PRESS
a capstone imprint

Pebble Plus is published by Capstone Press,
1710 Roe Crest Drive, North Mankato, Minnesota 56003.
www.capstonepub.com

Books published by Capstone Press are manufactured with paper
containing at least 10 percent post-consumer waste.

Library of Congress Cataloging-in-Publication Data
Hutmacher, Kimberly.
  I want a hamster / by Kimberly M. Hutmacher.
      p. cm.—(Pebble plus. I want a pet)
  Includes bibliographical references and index.
  Summary: "Simple text and full-color photographs describe the responsibilities involved in caring for and choosing
a hamster as a pet"—Provided by publisher.
  ISBN 978-1-4296-7598-7 (library binding)
  1. Hamsters—Juvenile literature. I. Title.
  QL737.R666H88 2012
  636.935'6—dc23   2011021653

Editorial Credits
Erika L. Shores, editor; Bobbie Nuytten, designer; Sarah Schuette, photo stylist; Marcy Morin, studio scheduler;
    Kathy McColley, production specialist

Photo Credits
All photos by Capstone Studio/Karon Dubke, except Shutterstock: Bartzuza, cover (top right), basel101658, cover (back)

Note to Parents and Teachers

The I Want a Pet series supports common core state standards for English language arts related
to reading informational text. This book describes and illustrates hamster ownership. The
images support early readers in understanding the text. The repetition of words and phrases
helps early readers learn new words. This book also introduces early readers to subject-specific
vocabulary words, which are defined in the Glossary section. Early readers may need assistance
to read some words and to use the Table of Contents, Glossary, Read More, Internet Sites, and
Index sections of the book.

Printed in the United States of America in North Mankato, Minnesota.
012013   007153R

Table of Contents

Hamsters Are for Me

A cute, cuddly hamster races
on its wheel. Would it be fun
to have a pet hamster?
What's involved in owning one?
Let's check out the responsibilities.

My Responsibilities

Hamsters live in cages

or large tanks called aquariums.

Do you have a spot in your house

to keep a hamster and its cage?

Hamsters need care every day. You'll feed it hamster food each night. Hamsters also like treats. You can give it pieces of apples or broccoli.

You'll have to clean your

hamster's cage once a week.

You'll take out old bedding.

Then wash the cage

and put in fresh bedding.

Hamsters can get sick.

If your hamster stops

eating or playing,

you'll take it to a veterinarian.

Choosing Your Hamster

Are you ready for

the responsibility?

You can buy hamsters

from pet stores or breeders.

Sorry, we CAN NOT rantee gender.

Look for a healthy hamster.

Listen for easy breathing.

It should have shiny fur,

clean eyes, and a clean bottom.

Buy food, dishes, water bottles,

bedding, and a cage.

Don't forget tubes for crawling

and wheels for running.

Hamsters need lots of exercise.

With good care, hamsters live
up to three years.
Care for your furry pet
and you'll have fun together
every day.

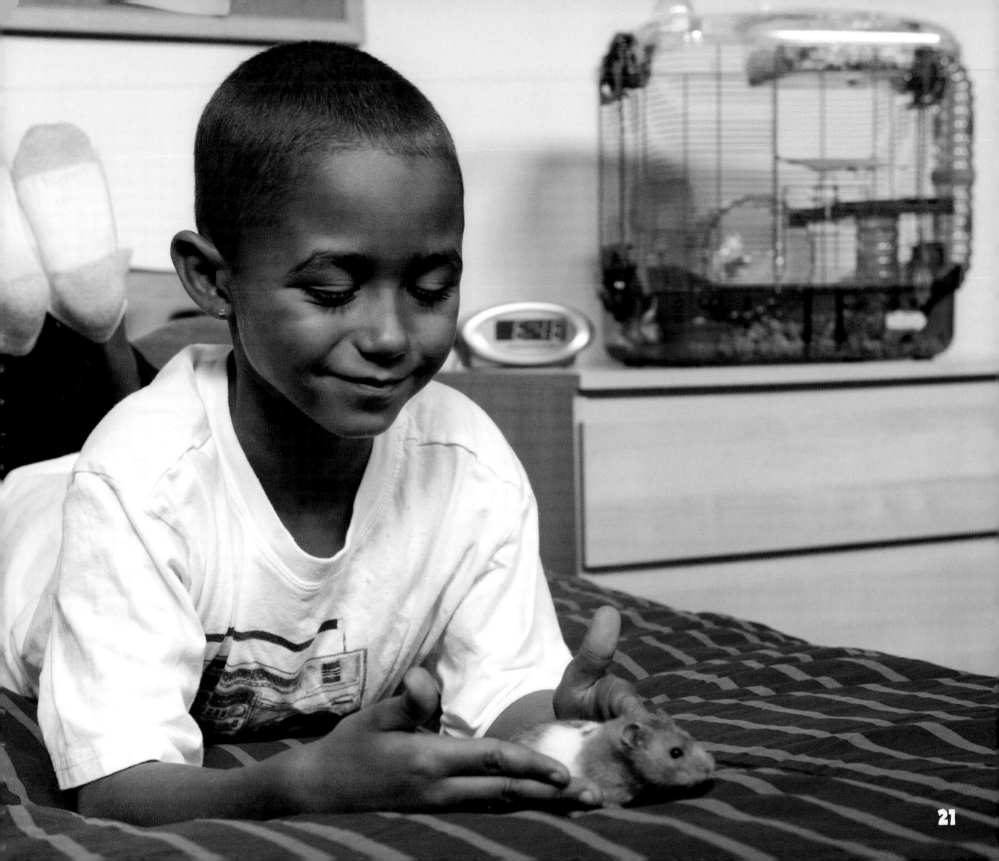

Glossary

aquarium—a glass or plastic tank where pets, including hamsters, hermit crabs, and fish, are kept

bedding—material used to make a bed; hamsters use wood shavings or shredded paper for bedding

breeder—a person who raises animals to sell

healthy—fit and well; not sick

responsibility—a duty or a job

veterinarian—a doctor who treats sick or injured animals; veterinarians also help animals stay healthy

Read More

Sabatés, Berta Garcia, and Mercè Segarra. *Let's Take Care of Our New Hamster.* Hauppauge, N.Y.: Barrons Educational Series, Inc., 2008.

Smalley, Carol Parenzan. *Care for a Pet Hamster.* How to Convince Your Parents You Can—. Hockessin, Del.: Mitchell Lane Publishers, 2010.

Zobel, Derek. *Caring for Your Hamster.* Pet Care Library. Minneapolis: Bellwether Media, 2011.

Internet Sites

FactHound offers a safe, fun way to find Internet sites related to this book. All of the sites on FactHound have been researched by our staff.

Here's all you do:

Visit *www.facthound.com*

Type in this code: 9781429675987

Super-cool stuff! Check out projects, games and lots more at **www.capstonekids.com**

Index

Word Count: 196
Grade: 1
Early-Intervention Level: 15